7 Businesses You Can Start Right Now, for Under $1000

By Elisabeth Miazello

Copyrights

© 2024 Elisabeth Miazello. All Rights Reserved.

This eBook is protected under the copyright laws of the United States and international treaties. No part of this book may be reproduced, distributed, or transmitted in any form or by any means, including photocopying, recording, or other electronic or mechanical methods, without the prior written permission of the author, except in the case of brief quotations embodied in critical reviews and certain other noncommercial uses permitted by copyright law.

Disclaimer

The information provided in this eBook is for general informational purposes only. All information in the eBook is provided in good faith, however, we make no representation or warranty of any kind, express or implied, regarding the accuracy, adequacy, validity, reliability, availability, or completeness of any information in the eBook. Under no circumstance shall we have any liability to you for any loss or damage of any kind incurred as a result of the use of the eBook or reliance on any information provided in the eBook. Your use of the eBook and your reliance on any information in the eBook is solely at your own risk.

Dear Reader,

Thank you for downloading and reading "**7 Businesses You Can Start Right Now for Under $1000.**" I hope this guide has provided you with the inspiration and practical advice needed to kickstart your entrepreneurial journey.

Creating this book was a labor of love, aimed at empowering individuals like you to break free from the 9-5 grind and achieve financial freedom through smart, low-cost business strategies. Your support means the world to me, and I am grateful for the opportunity to share these insights with you.

If you found this book helpful and inspiring, I would be incredibly grateful if you could take a moment to leave a review on Amazon. Your feedback helps other aspiring entrepreneurs discover this resource and benefit from the strategies and examples shared within these pages.

Author Page

To leave a review on Amazon, just scan the code above or visit:

Elisabeth Miazello Amazon Profile:
https://www.amazon.com/author/elisabeth.miazello

Thank you once again for your support and for being a part of this journey. Wishing you all the best in your path to financial freedom and entrepreneurial success.

With gratitude,
Elisabeth Miazello

Ready to Transform Your Future?

Grab your **FREE eBook** now and discover:

7 Businesses to Avoid and 4 Winning Opportunities: Your Business Success Guide.

Don't miss out on this opportunity to kickstart your entrepreneurial journey!

Scan the **QR Code** Above or Visit **IRNOX.com/7c** for an Instant Free Download

Take the first step towards financial freedom.

Table of Contents:

Introduction 6
Chapter 1: 9
The Foundations of High ROI, Low-Cash Businesses .. 9
Chapter 2: 13
The Business Matrix - SELL 13
Chapter 3: 18
Remote Window Cleaning Business 18
Chapter 4: 24
Real Estate Listing Video Editor 24
Chapter 5: 30
Microgreens Business 30
Chapter 6: 36
Wedding Arches and Decorations Rental 36
Chapter 7: 42
Handyman Services 42
Chapter 8: 48
Virtual Assistant Company 48
Chapter 9: 54
Productized Services 54
Conclusion 60

Introduction

Hey there! Welcome to "**7 Businesses You Can Start Right Now for Under $1000.**" If you're here, you're probably dreaming of breaking free from the 9-5 grind and building a life where you call the shots. You're in the right place because this book is all about making that dream a reality with smart, low-cost business strategies.

Why This Book?

Let's face it, starting a business can be daunting, especially if you're strapped for cash. But here's the good news: You don't need a fortune to kickstart your entrepreneurial journey. We're talking about high ROI, low-cash businesses that can bring in serious money without breaking the bank. We'll dive into real-world examples, practical advice, and proven strategies to help you start your own successful business.

What is High ROI, Low-Cash Business?

In plain English, it's about how much money you make compared to how much you spend. We're looking for businesses that give you a big bang for your buck—lots of income with minimal upfront costs.

Now, we also factor in the investment length—how long it takes to see returns. We want businesses that start making money quickly because who has time to wait years for a payoff?

Why Avoid Traditional Investments?

You might be wondering why we're not suggesting putting your money into stocks, crypto, or real estate. Simple: If you're working with a limited budget, these investments don't give you the immediate returns you need. Stocks might give you a 10% return over a year, but that's $100 on a $1,000 investment—not exactly life-changing. Real estate? Even less practical with high entry costs and slow returns.

Instead, we'll focus on businesses you can start with little money down but have the potential to generate significant income fast.

The Business Matrix - SELL

To guide you in choosing the right business, we use what we call the **SELL** matrix:

- **S**ellable: You can sell a product or service right away.
- **E**arning Potential: The business can make at least $100K a year.
- **L**ow Cost: Start with less than $1,000.
- **L**everage: You can outsource much of the work.

We'll show you seven businesses that tick all these boxes and more.

The Journey Ahead

Throughout this book, you'll find actionable advice and real-world examples to inspire and guide you. From remote window cleaning to renting out wedding decorations, each chapter is packed with insights and strategies to help you start and grow your own successful business.

So, are you ready to take the first step towards financial freedom? Let's dive in and discover the amazing opportunities waiting for you!

Chapter 1:
The Foundations of High ROI, Low-Cash Businesses

Hey there! Ready to dive into the world of high ROI, low-cash businesses? Great! Let's get started by laying down some essential foundations. Understanding these basics will set you up for success as we explore different business opportunities.

What is ROI?

First things first, let's talk about ROI—Return on Investment. ROI is a way to measure how much money you're making compared to how much you're spending. It's super important for any business, especially when you're starting with limited funds.

In simple terms, ROI tells you the percentage of profit you've made on your investment. For example, if you spend $1,000 to start a business and make $10,000, your ROI is 900%. Pretty impressive, right?

Importance of Investment Length

ROI is crucial, but we also need to consider how long it takes to see those returns. This is where investment length comes in. The shorter the time to see your profits, the better. We want businesses that start making money quickly, not ones that take years to pay off.

Think of it this way: Would you rather wait a year to make $1,000 or make that same amount in a month? Exactly. Faster returns mean you can reinvest sooner and grow your business more quickly.

Why Avoid Traditional Investments?

Now, you might be thinking, "Why not just invest in stocks, crypto, or real estate?" Well, here's the deal: Traditional investments usually require a lot of money upfront and take time to see significant returns. Let's break it down:

- **Stocks:** On average, stocks return about 10% per year. So, if you invest $1,000, you might make $100 after a year. Not bad, but not great if you're looking to make substantial money quickly.

- **Crypto:** While crypto can offer high returns, it's also highly volatile. You could make a lot or lose everything. It's a risky game, especially with limited funds.

- **Real Estate:** Real estate investments can be lucrative, but they require significant capital and time. A $1,000 investment won't get you far in the real estate market.

Instead, we focus on high ROI, low-cash businesses. These businesses require minimal upfront investment and have the potential to generate substantial income quickly.

Introducing the SELL Matrix

To help you identify the right business opportunities, we've developed the SELL matrix. This handy tool will guide you in choosing businesses that are:

- ****S**ellable:** You can start selling products or services from day one.
- ****E**arning Potential:** The business has the potential to make at least $100K a year.
- ****L**ow Cost:** You can start the business with less than $1,000.
- ****L**everage:** You can outsource much of the work, so you're not tied down to doing everything yourself.

We'll be using the SELL matrix throughout this book to evaluate different business ideas. This way, you'll know exactly what to look for and how to determine if a business is right for you.

The Power of Doing the Work

One more thing before we dive into specific business ideas: You have to do the work. There's no shortcut to success. Building a business takes effort, dedication, and a willingness to tackle challenges head-on.

Remember, "life hack: always the stairs, never the elevator." The hard work you put in now will pay off later. By committing to doing the necessary work, you'll set yourself apart from those who just talk about starting a business but never act.

Chapter 2:
The Business Matrix - SELL

Alright, now that we've got the basics down, let's jump into the Business Matrix that will guide us through identifying and evaluating the best business opportunities. We call this the SELL matrix. Why SELL? Because we want businesses that can sell products or services effectively and meet our criteria for success.

What is the SELL Matrix?

The SELL matrix stands for:

- **S**ellable: Can you start selling a product or service from day one?
- **E**arning Potential: Can the business make at least $100K a year?
- **L**ow Cost: Can you start the business with less than $1,000?
- **L**everage: Can you outsource much of the work?

This matrix will be our roadmap, helping us evaluate business ideas to ensure they meet our goals of high

ROI, low upfront cost, and quick returns. Let's break it down further.

Sellable: Get Selling from Day One

The first criterion is sellable. We want businesses that allow you to start selling right away. No long development times, no endless preparation—just straight to market.

Think about a lemonade stand: simple, straightforward, and ready to start making money immediately. We're looking for business ideas that you can kick off quickly, providing a service or product that people need and are willing to pay for right now.

Earning Potential: Aim High

Next up is earning potential. We're not just looking for side hustles here; we want businesses that can bring in serious cash. The goal is to make at least $100K a year. Why? Because this level of income can truly change your life, giving you financial freedom and the ability to reinvest in your business for even more growth.

Imagine the possibilities: paying off debt, saving for the future, or even taking that dream vacation. A high-earning business makes all these things possible.

Low Cost: Start Small, Grow Big

We're all about low-cost startups. You shouldn't need to empty your savings or take out massive loans to get started. Each business idea we explore will require an initial investment of less than $1,000.

Low-cost doesn't mean low quality or low potential. It means smart investing—using your resources wisely to create a solid foundation for your business. We'll show you how to start small and scale up, maximizing every dollar you spend.

Leverage: Work Smarter, Not Harder

Finally, we come to leverage. One of the keys to a successful business is being able to outsource tasks. You don't want to be doing everything yourself—that's a fast track to burnout. Instead, we look for businesses where you can delegate work to others, allowing you to focus on growing the business.

Think about it: the more you can outsource, the more time you have to strategize, innovate, and scale. Leverage is all about working smarter, not harder.

Applying the SELL Matrix

Now that we understand what the SELL matrix is, let's see it in action. We'll use this framework to evaluate each business idea we cover in the upcoming chapters. Here's a quick preview:

1. **Remote Window Cleaning Business:** Low startup costs, high earning potential, and the ability to outsource.
2. **Real Estate Listing Video Editor:** High demand, minimal investment, and straightforward to scale.
3. **Microgreens Business:** High profitability, easy to start with low costs, and scalable with outsourcing.
4. **Wedding Arches and Decorations Rental:** Profitable market with room for upsells and scalable through smart marketing.
5. **Handyman Services:** Essential services with high demand, low startup costs, and potential for outsourcing.
6. **Virtual Assistant Company:** Low cost, high margin, and entirely based on leveraging other people's skills.

7. **Productized Services:** Recurring revenue with a subscription model, easy to start, and scalable through outsourcing.

In each chapter, we'll dive deep into one of these business models, applying the SELL matrix to show you exactly why they work and how you can start. We'll provide actionable steps, real-world examples, and tips to help you succeed.

Chapter 3:
Remote Window Cleaning Business

Welcome to the first business opportunity in our lineup: Remote Window Cleaning. This might sound simple, but it's a powerhouse when it comes to high ROI and low startup costs. Let's dive in and see why this business fits perfectly into our SELL matrix.

Why Remote Window Cleaning?

You might be thinking, "Window cleaning? Really?" Yes, really. This business is straightforward, has minimal startup costs, and can be highly profitable. Plus, you can easily outsource the actual cleaning work while you focus on growing the business. Let's break it down.

Sellable: Get Started Today

The beauty of window cleaning is that it's immediately sellable. People always need their windows cleaned—whether it's homes, offices, or stores. You don't need months of preparation. A quick investment in some basic equipment, and you're ready to start.

Imagine this: A couple of days after setting up, you're already cleaning your first windows and making money. It's that fast.

Earning Potential: High Returns with Low Costs

Let's talk numbers. You can charge anywhere from $100 to $500 per job. If you add services like pressure washing, you can charge even more. Here's a real-world example: Johnny, a 19-year-old entrepreneur, built a $20,000/month remote window cleaning business.

Johnny's story shows us how this works. He started small, targeting big houses and stores, and scaled up by outsourcing the cleaning work. He focused on getting clients while subcontractors did the cleaning.

Low Cost: Minimal Investment, Big Gains

The startup costs for a window cleaning business are incredibly low. Here's what you'll need:

- Accessories: $40
- Ladder: $80
- Hose: $40
- Cleaning solution: $20

Even if you scale up, your initial investment might be around $1,800. Compare this to other businesses, and you'll see why window cleaning is a fantastic low-cost startup.

Leverage: Outsource and Scale

One of the best parts about this business is the ability to outsource. You don't have to clean the windows yourself. Instead, you can hire subcontractors. This approach is what allowed Johnny to scale his business so quickly.

Here's how Johnny did it:

1. **Getting Customers:** He used Google Ads, TikTok, Instagram, and local SEO to attract clients. Most people search online for window cleaners, so having a strong online presence is crucial.

2. **Outsourcing the Work:** Johnny didn't do the cleaning himself. He connected with other window cleaning businesses and offered them leads in exchange for a percentage of the earnings. This way, he leveraged his marketing skills and let others handle the labor.

3. **Quality Assurance:** To ensure high-quality service, Johnny used Booking Koala to manage bookings and follow up with clients to get reviews. This helped him build a strong reputation and attract even more customers.

Johnny's success story is inspiring. Starting with less than $1,000, he grew his business to earn $20,000 a month. By focusing on getting clients and outsourcing the work, he scaled quickly and efficiently.

Actionable Steps to Start Your Own Remote Window Cleaning Business

Ready to get started? Here's a step-by-step guide:

1. **Buy Basic Equipment:** Start with essential tools like a ladder, hose, cleaning solutions, and accessories. You can find these at local stores or online.

2. **Set Up Online Presence:** Create a simple website and social media accounts. Use platforms like Google Ads and social media to attract clients.

3. **Network with Subcontractors:** Reach out to local window cleaning businesses and offer to provide them with leads in exchange for a commission. Use local Facebook groups, trade associations, and Google to find potential partners.

4. **Focus on Customer Reviews:** Encourage your clients to leave reviews. Use tools like Booking Koala to manage bookings and follow-ups. Offer small incentives to your subcontractors for getting reviews.

5. **Scale Up:** As you get more clients, continue to outsource the cleaning work. Focus on

expanding your marketing efforts and managing customer relationships.

Starting a remote window cleaning business is a fantastic way to dive into entrepreneurship. With low startup costs, high earning potential, and the ability to leverage other people's labor, it's a smart, scalable business model.

Chapter 4:
Real Estate Listing Video Editor

Welcome to another fantastic business opportunity: Real Estate Listing Video Editor. This one's a gem, especially in today's market where visuals are everything. Let's dive into why this business is a goldmine and how you can start making money with minimal investment.

Why Real Estate Listing Video Editing?

Real estate is a competitive field, and agents are always looking for ways to make their listings stand out. That's where you come in. By offering video editing services, you can help real estate agents attract more buyers and close deals faster. It's a high-demand service with low startup costs and significant earning potential.

Sellable: Ready to Start Immediately

Video editing is a service you can start offering right away. Real estate agents need polished, professional videos to showcase properties, and you can provide that service from day one. No need for lengthy setup times or complex preparations.

Picture this: Within a week of setting up your business, you could be editing your first real estate video and getting paid. It's that quick and straightforward.

Earning Potential: High Demand, High Returns

Let's talk about the money. Real estate agents are willing to pay good money for quality videos because they know it helps them sell properties faster. You can charge anywhere from $50 to $150 per video, depending on the complexity and your experience.

Take Sam, for example. Before working full-time for me, Sam ran his own real estate video editing business and made $100,000 a year. The demand for his services was so high that he couldn't keep up, which shows just how lucrative this business can be.

Low Cost: Start with What You Have

The beauty of this business is that you don't need a lot of fancy equipment to get started. Here's what you'll need:

- **Computer:** You probably already have one.
- **Video Editing Software:** There are plenty of affordable options, like Adobe Premiere

Pro or even free software like DaVinci Resolve.
- **Basic Camera:** Optional, as many agents will provide the footage.

You can start with just your computer and editing software, making the initial investment incredibly low.

Leverage: Outsource and Grow

As your business grows, you can start outsourcing parts of the work. Hire other video editors to handle some of the editing, allowing you to take on more clients and focus on expanding your business.

Here's how Sam did it:

1. **Learning the Basics:** Sam spent a few hours learning how to clip videos together. He didn't need to become a Hollywood-level editor, just proficient enough to create appealing real estate videos.

2. **Finding Clients:** He reached out to real estate agents on Zillow and Redfin, offering to create sample videos for them. Once they saw the quality of his work, they were eager to hire him.

3. **Scaling the Business:** As demand grew, Sam hired additional editors to help with the workload. This allowed him to take on more clients and increase his earnings.

Sam's story is a testament to how lucrative and scalable this business can be. By starting with minimal investment and leveraging his skills, he built a business that generated $100,000 a year. And when he moved on, his fiancée took over and continued to grow the business, proving its sustainability.

Actionable Steps to Start Your Own Real Estate Listing Video Editing Business

Ready to jump in? Here's a step-by-step guide:

1. **Learn Basic Video Editing:** Spend a week learning how to edit videos using software like Adobe Premiere Pro or DaVinci Resolve. There are plenty of tutorials available online.

2. **Create Sample Videos:** Use stock footage or real estate listings you find online to create a portfolio of sample videos. This will help you showcase your skills to potential clients.

3. **Reach Out to Real Estate Agents:** Contact agents on Zillow, Redfin, and other real estate platforms. Offer to create a sample video for their listings to demonstrate your value.

4. **Set Up Your Online Presence:** Create a simple website and social media profiles to showcase your portfolio and attract clients. Use SEO and social media marketing to reach a wider audience.

5. **Start Taking Clients:** Once you land your first few clients, focus on delivering high-quality work and building a reputation. Encourage satisfied clients to leave reviews and refer you to others.

6. **Scale Up:** As your client base grows, consider hiring additional editors to handle the workload.

This will allow you to take on more clients and increase your earnings.

Starting a real estate listing video editing business is a fantastic way to leverage your skills and make a significant income with minimal investment. With high demand and the ability to scale, it's a smart choice for aspiring entrepreneurs.

Chapter 5:
Microgreens Business

Welcome to another exciting business opportunity: growing and selling microgreens. This one's for all the green thumbs out there—or even those who've never gardened before but want to try something new and profitable. Let's explore why microgreens are a fantastic high ROI, low-cash business and how you can get started.

Why Microgreens?

Microgreens are young plants, harvested just after they've sprouted. They're packed with nutrients and have become incredibly popular in the culinary world. Chefs love them for their flavor and health benefits, and consumers are willing to pay a premium for fresh, locally-grown greens. This makes microgreens a high-demand product that's easy to grow and sell.

Sellable: Start Selling Quickly

Microgreens are sellable almost immediately. With a growing cycle of just a few weeks, you can start selling your first crop within a month. This quick turnaround means you can begin making money fast, without a long wait.

Imagine this: In just 30 days, you could be harvesting your first batch of microgreens and selling them to local restaurants, farmers markets, or even directly to consumers through online platforms. It's that straightforward.

Earning Potential: High Profit Margins

Microgreens are known for their high profitability. Let's break down the numbers. Jonah, a successful microgreens entrepreneur, started with less than $700 and made $60,000 in his first year. By scaling up his operation, he later earned $700,000 annually with healthy profit margins.

Here's how it works: For every six-foot plant rack you set up, you can generate around $2,000 in revenue per cycle. Initially, you'll keep about 85% of that as profit because you'll be doing most of the work yourself. As you scale and potentially outsource parts of the operation, your margins might decrease slightly but your overall revenue will increase.

Low Cost: Affordable Startup

Starting a microgreens business doesn't require a hefty investment. Here's a basic cost breakdown:

- Plant Rack: $100
- Seeds: $50
- Growing Medium: $50
- Lighting: $100
- Miscellaneous Supplies: $50

That's a total of around $350 to get started. You can expand as your business grows, adding more racks and increasing your production capacity.

Leverage: Outsource and Expand

Once you get the hang of growing microgreens, you can start thinking about how to leverage your time and resources. Hiring help for tasks like planting, harvesting, and packing can free up your time to focus on expanding your market and growing your business.

Jonah's success didn't just come from his green thumb. He used smart business strategies to scale. Here's how:

1. **Find Your Space:** Start with a small, indoor space. This could be a spare room, basement, or even a closet with proper lighting. You don't need a lot of space to get started.

2. **Buy Equipment:** Get your racks, lights, seeds, and growing medium. You can find these supplies at gardening stores or online.

3. **Start Growing:** Follow simple guides to start growing your microgreens. It takes about 2-3 weeks for a crop to be ready for harvest. Use software like VertiGrow to manage your plant rotation and watering schedules.

4. **Find Customers:** Start by selling directly to consumers at farmers markets or through Facebook Marketplace. Reach out to local restaurants and grocery stores. Many chefs are willing to pay a premium for fresh, local microgreens.

5. **Create a Subscription Model:** Offer a subscription service for regular deliveries. This provides a steady stream of income and builds a loyal customer base.

Jonah's journey is a testament to how profitable and scalable the microgreens business can be. Starting with just a few hundred dollars, he built a thriving business by consistently producing high-quality greens and finding reliable customers. His story shows that with dedication and smart strategies, you can achieve significant success.

Actionable Steps to Start Your Own Microgreens Business

Ready to get growing? Here's a step-by-step guide:

1. **Set Up Your Growing Space:** Find a suitable indoor space and set up your plant racks and lights. Ensure the environment is controlled for temperature and humidity.

2. **Get Your Supplies:** Purchase seeds, growing medium, and other necessary supplies. Start with easy-to-grow varieties like radishes, broccoli, and sunflower.

3. **Start Growing:** Plant your seeds and follow a regular watering schedule. Monitor the growth and adjust conditions as needed to ensure healthy plants.

4. **Harvest and Pack:** Once your microgreens are ready, harvest them carefully and pack them for sale. Use eco-friendly packaging to appeal to health-conscious customers.

5. **Market Your Greens:** Create a simple website and social media profiles to showcase your products. Attend farmers markets, reach out to local restaurants, and consider offering a subscription service.

6. **Scale Up:** As you gain experience and customers, invest in more racks and consider hiring help. Focus on expanding your market and increasing your production capacity.

Starting a microgreens business is a fantastic way to combine your love for gardening with a profitable venture. With low startup costs, high earning potential, and the ability to scale, it's an excellent choice for aspiring entrepreneurs.

Chapter 6:
Wedding Arches and Decorations Rental

Let's dive into a business that's not just beautiful but also highly profitable: renting wedding arches and decorations. Weddings are a big deal, and people are willing to spend a lot to make their special day perfect. This business taps into that desire, offering high returns for a relatively low investment. Ready to make some magic happen? Let's go!

Why Wedding Arches and Decorations?

Weddings are emotional events, and couples often go all out to create the perfect setting. This means they're willing to spend big bucks on decorations. By renting out wedding arches and other decorations, you can provide a valuable service without needing a massive initial investment. Plus, these items can be reused, maximizing your profits over time.

Sellable: Hit the Ground Running

Wedding arches and decorations are in demand year-round. With wedding seasons in spring and summer, plus engagements and anniversaries, you have plenty of opportunities to rent out your inventory. The best part?

Once you purchase your initial stock, you can start renting it out almost immediately.

Imagine this: You invest in a few beautiful arches and some decorations, and within weeks, you're booking your first rental. It's a quick way to start generating income.

Earning Potential: High Profits, Recurring Revenue

Let's break down the potential earnings. Jimmy, an entrepreneur in this space, noticed that less than 22% of weddings take place indoors, creating a huge market for mobile marriage supplies. He invested $2,200 in tents and charged $500 per gig. After just four rentals, he had covered his initial costs.

For wedding arches and accessories, here's a simple cost breakdown:

- Arches and Accessories: $1,100
- Additional Decorations and Upsell Items: $1,200

   Total initial investment: $2,300

Now, let's look at the revenue. By charging $1,500 per rental (including upsells), and doing just 60 rentals a year (roughly one per weekend), you're looking at $90,000 annually. Add tents and other accessories, and you can easily push your earnings to $180,000 or more.

Low Cost: Affordable to Start

Starting this business won't break the bank. With an initial investment of around $2,300, you can get the essentials to start renting out wedding arches and decorations. Here's what you'll need:

- Wedding Arch: $300
- Decorative Items (Flowers, Drapes, etc.): $500
- Additional Accessories (Lights, Seating, etc.): $1,000
- Transport and Setup Costs: $500

You can start small and expand your inventory as your business grows.

Leverage: Outsource and Simplify

Once you've got your inventory and a few rentals under your belt, you can think about leveraging your time and resources. Outsourcing the setup and breakdown of decorations can free you up to handle more clients and focus on expanding your business.

Here's how Jimmy did it:

1. **Identify Your Market:** Jimmy focused on local weddings and events. He reached out to wedding planners, offering them a commission for every client they referred to him. This partnership approach quickly expanded his client base.

2. **Create a Simple Website:** Jimmy built a basic website showcasing his arches and decorations. He included pricing and contact information, making it easy for potential clients to see what he offered and book his services.

3. **Use Social Media:** By posting beautiful photos of his decorations on Instagram and Facebook, Jimmy attracted more clients. He also joined local wedding groups and forums to network and promote his business.

4. **Network with Wedding Planners:** Wedding planners are always looking for reliable vendors. By building relationships with them, Jimmy ensured a steady stream of referrals.

5. **Offer Customization:** Each wedding is unique, so Jimmy offered customization options. This not only appealed to clients but also allowed him to charge premium prices.

Jimmy's story is a perfect example of how a small investment can lead to substantial profits. By focusing on local markets, leveraging partnerships, and offering customization, he built a business that generated $180,000 annually. His approach was simple but effective, proving that with the right strategy, you can achieve significant success.

Actionable Steps to Start Your Own Wedding Arches and Decorations Rental Business

Ready to get started? Here's a step-by-step guide:

1. **Purchase Initial Inventory:** Start with a few high-quality wedding arches and decorative items. Focus on pieces that are versatile and can be customized for different themes.

2. **Set Up Your Online Presence:** Create a simple website and social media profiles. Showcase your inventory with professional photos and detailed descriptions.

3. **Network with Wedding Planners:** Reach out to local wedding planners and offer them a commission for referrals. Attend wedding fairs and events to make connections.

4. **Offer Customization:** Provide options for customizing the decorations to meet different clients' needs. This can set you apart from competitors and justify higher prices.

5. **Market Aggressively:** Use social media, Google Ads, and local advertising to promote your business. Highlight your unique selling points and showcase client testimonials.

6. **Scale Up:** As your business grows, reinvest profits into expanding your inventory. Consider hiring staff or subcontractors to handle setup and breakdown, allowing you to take on more clients.

Starting a wedding arches and decorations rental business is a fantastic way to tap into a lucrative market with high demand and emotional appeal.

Chapter 7:
Handyman Services

Let's dive into a business that combines practicality with profitability: handyman services. If you're good with tools and love fixing things, this business can be a goldmine. And if you're not handy, don't worry—you can still succeed by outsourcing the work. Ready to turn everyday skills into a thriving business? Let's get started!

Why Handyman Services?

Handyman services are always in demand. From fixing leaky faucets to painting walls and assembling furniture, there's no shortage of tasks that homeowners and businesses need help with. This makes it a versatile and steady business opportunity with high earning potential and low startup costs.

Sellable: Easy to Market

Handyman services are immediately sellable. Everyone needs repairs and maintenance, but not everyone has the time or skills to do it themselves. You can start marketing your services right away and begin booking jobs within days.

Imagine this: You put up a few flyers in your neighborhood, post an ad online, and within a week, you're getting calls from people who need help with various tasks. It's a quick and effective way to start making money.

Earning Potential: High Demand, High Returns

Let's talk about the financial side. Caleb Ingram, an entrepreneur who started his own handyman business, makes $250,000 a year. How? By charging $100 to $200 per hour for his services and keeping his costs low. Here's a breakdown of what's possible:

- Hourly Rate: $100 to $200
- Average Job: 2-3 hours
- Weekly Jobs: 10-15

With these numbers, you can easily see how Caleb reached his impressive income. And remember, you don't have to do all the work yourself. By outsourcing to subcontractors, you can manage multiple jobs simultaneously, increasing your revenue.

Low Cost: Minimal Investment

Starting a handyman business doesn't require a significant investment. Most of the tools you need can be found in your garage or bought second-hand. Here's what you'll need:

- **Basic Tools:** $200-$500 (drill, hammer, screwdrivers, wrenches, etc.)
- **Marketing:** $100-$200 (flyers, business cards, online ads)
- **Transportation:** Use your own vehicle

For less than $1,000, you can have everything you need to start offering handyman services. And as you earn, you can reinvest in more specialized tools to expand your services.

Leverage: Outsource and Expand

One of the keys to scaling a handyman business is leveraging your time. By outsourcing tasks to subcontractors, you can take on more jobs and focus on growing your business. This is how Caleb managed to build a six-figure business without getting overwhelmed.

Here's how Caleb did it:

1. **Niche Down to a Neighborhood:** Caleb focused on Northern Seattle, his local area, to reduce travel costs and build a strong local reputation. This helped him rank on the first page of Google for local searches.

2. **Obsess Over Reviews:** Reviews are crucial for a service-based business. Caleb used a system like Jobber to encourage customers to leave reviews. Offering small bonuses to subcontractors for getting reviews also helped build his online presence.

3. **Add Subcontractors:** To scale, Caleb hired subcontractors to handle the physical work. This allowed him to focus on marketing, client relationships, and expanding his service offerings.

Caleb's story is a perfect example of turning everyday skills into a thriving business. By starting small, focusing on customer satisfaction, and leveraging subcontractors, he built a business that generates $250,000 a year. His success shows that with the right approach, you can achieve significant financial freedom.

Actionable Steps to Start Your Own Handyman Services Business

Ready to get started? Here's a step-by-step guide:

1. **Gather Your Tools:** Start with basic tools that you likely already have. Invest in additional tools as needed based on the jobs you take on.

2. **Create a Business Plan:** Outline the services you'll offer, pricing, and target market. A clear plan will help you stay focused and organized.

3. **Market Your Services:** Use local advertising, social media, and word of mouth to attract clients. Create a simple website and list your services on local directories like Yelp and Google My Business.

4. **Focus on Customer Reviews:** Encourage every customer to leave a review. Offer small incentives to subcontractors for getting reviews, and use a system like Jobber to streamline the process.

5. **Hire Subcontractors:** As demand grows, start outsourcing tasks to subcontractors. This will allow you to handle more jobs and focus on growing your business.

6. **Scale Up:** As your business grows, invest in more tools and expand your service offerings. Consider hiring a full-time team to handle larger projects and increase your capacity.

Starting a handyman services business is a practical and profitable way to leverage your skills. With high demand, low startup costs, and the ability to scale through outsourcing.

Chapter 8:
Virtual Assistant Company

Now, let's explore a business opportunity that takes advantage of the global workforce and the rise of remote work: starting a virtual assistant (VA) company. This business model is all about connecting businesses with skilled assistants from around the world. With minimal startup costs and high earning potential, it's a fantastic option for aspiring entrepreneurs. Ready to dive in? Let's get started!

Why a Virtual Assistant Company?

Virtual assistant services are in high demand as businesses look for cost-effective ways to handle administrative tasks, customer support, social media management, and more. By starting a VA company, you can tap into this demand and offer valuable services without the need for a large initial investment.

Sellable: Immediate Demand

The demand for virtual assistants is growing rapidly. Businesses and entrepreneurs are constantly looking for help with day-to-day tasks that don't require a full-time employee. By positioning yourself as the go-to provider for these services, you can start acquiring clients right away.

Imagine this: Within a month of starting your VA company, you could have multiple clients, each paying you a steady monthly fee. It's a quick way to establish a reliable income stream.

Earning Potential: High Margins, Recurring Revenue

Let's break down the earning potential. A well-run VA company can bring in significant revenue with high profit margins. Here's a look at how you can structure your pricing:

- Monthly Retainer: $1,500 to $10,000 per client, depending on the services provided and the number of hours required.
- Placement Fee: Charge $3,000 to $5,000 for finding and placing a VA with a client.

Consider this example: You assist me, a successful VA company, generates millions in revenue annually. By charging competitive rates and maintaining a roster of skilled VAs, you can achieve similar success.

Low Cost: Minimal Startup Investment

Starting a VA company requires very little upfront investment. Here's what you'll need:

- **Website:** $100-$200 for a basic site.
- **Marketing:** $200-$500 for initial advertising and outreach.
- **Communication Tools:** Use free or low-cost tools like Zoom, Slack, and Trello.

For less than $1,000, you can have your VA company up and running.

Leverage: Outsource and Scale

The beauty of a VA company is that you're leveraging other people's skills and time. You're the middleman, connecting businesses with virtual assistants. This allows you to scale your business quickly without being bogged down by the actual work.

Here's how successful VA companies operate:

1. **Find Clients:** Reach out to businesses and entrepreneurs who could benefit from a VA. Use platforms like LinkedIn, Twitter, and business forums to connect with potential clients.

2. **Outsource Talent:** Use platforms like Upwork and Fiverr to find skilled virtual assistants. Screen candidates carefully to ensure they meet your clients' needs.

3. **Maintain Quality Control:** Regularly check in with both clients and VAs to ensure everything is running smoothly. Provide ongoing support and training to your VAs to keep them performing at their best.

Consider companies like Support Shepherd and You Assist Me. These businesses started with minimal investment and have grown into multi-million-dollar operations. By focusing on quality service, effective marketing, and efficient management, they've built strong reputations and loyal client bases.

Actionable Steps to Start Your Own Virtual Assistant Company

Ready to build your VA empire? Here's a step-by-step guide:

1. **Set Up Your Website:** Create a professional website that outlines your services, pricing, and contact information. Include testimonials and case studies to build credibility.

2. **Identify Your Niche:** Decide what types of services your VAs will specialize in. This could be general administrative tasks, social media management, customer support, or industry-specific tasks.

3. **Find Clients:** Start with your network. Reach out to business owners and entrepreneurs who might need VA services. Use LinkedIn, Twitter, and business forums to connect with potential clients.

4. **Recruit VAs:** Use platforms like Upwork, Fiverr, and LinkedIn to find skilled virtual assistants. Screen candidates thoroughly and create a pool of reliable VAs ready to work.

5. **Set Your Pricing:** Decide on your pricing model. Consider offering both monthly retainers and placement fees. Ensure your rates cover your costs and provide a healthy profit margin.

6. **Market Your Services:** Use social media, online ads, and content marketing to promote your VA company. Highlight the benefits of using VAs and showcase your success stories.

7. **Scale Up:** As you acquire more clients, hire additional VAs and consider bringing on team members to help with client management and quality control.

Starting a virtual assistant company is a smart way to tap into the growing demand for remote work and outsourced services.

Chapter 9:
Productized Services

Now, let's explore a business model that can turn your skills into a scalable, multi-million-dollar enterprise: productized services. This model is all about offering a specialized service on a subscription basis, providing consistent revenue and the potential for significant growth. Ready to learn how to turn your expertise into a thriving business? Let's dive in!

Why Productized Services?

Productized services take a specific skill or service and package it into a standardized offering that clients can subscribe to. This model simplifies your service delivery, creates predictable income, and allows you to scale by leveraging technology and outsourcing.

Imagine this: You offer a specialized service, like graphic design or video editing, on a monthly subscription basis. Clients pay a flat fee and get access to your services as needed. This creates a steady stream of income and allows you to focus on delivering quality work without constantly chasing new clients.

Sellable: Easy to Market and Scale

Productized services are highly sellable because they offer clients convenience and predictability. Clients know exactly what they're getting and can budget for it easily. Plus, the subscription model creates recurring revenue, making it easier for you to plan and grow your business.

Picture this: Within a few weeks of launching your productized service, you could have several clients on monthly subscriptions, providing you with a reliable income stream.

Earning Potential: High Revenue, Low Overhead

Let's break down the earning potential. Brett Williams, a graphic designer, turned his skill into a productized service called Design Joy. He offers unlimited graphic design requests on a subscription basis and generates $1.3 million annually. Here's how:

- Monthly Subscription: Clients pay a flat fee, typically around $1,000 to $5,000 per month, for unlimited design requests.
- Scalable Model: By using a standardized process and outsourcing some tasks, Brett manages to handle multiple clients efficiently.

With this model, you can scale your business quickly. The more clients you add, the more revenue you generate, all while keeping your overhead low by leveraging technology and outsourcing.

Low Cost: Affordable to Start

Starting a productized service business doesn't require a significant investment. Here's what you'll need:

- Website: $100-$200 for a professional site.
- Marketing: $200-$500 for initial advertising and outreach.
- Tools: Depending on your service, you might need software subscriptions (e.g., Adobe Creative Suite for design services).

For less than $1,000, you can launch your productized service and start attracting clients.

Leverage: Outsource and Automate

The key to scaling a productized service is leveraging your time and resources. By outsourcing tasks and using automation tools, you can handle more clients without increasing your workload significantly.

Here's how Brett did it:

1. **Standardize Your Service:** Define exactly what you offer and create a clear process for delivering your service. This helps ensure consistency and efficiency.

2. **Automate Onboarding:** Use tools to automate the client onboarding process. This could include automated emails, online forms, and a client portal where clients can submit requests.

3. **Outsource Tasks:** Hire freelancers or contractors to handle specific tasks. For example, Brett outsources some design tasks to other designers, allowing him to manage more clients.

4. **Focus on Customer Experience:** Ensure that your clients have a seamless experience. Use feedback to continuously improve your service and maintain high client satisfaction.

Brett's story is a perfect example of how a productized service can turn a skill into a million-dollar business. By standardizing his graphic design service and offering it on a subscription basis, he created a scalable business model that generates $1.3 million annually. His success shows that with the right approach, you can achieve significant growth and financial freedom.

Actionable Steps to Start Your Own Productized Service Business

Ready to get started? Here's a step-by-step guide:

1. **Identify Your Skill:** Choose a skill or service that you can standardize and offer on a subscription basis. This could be graphic design, video editing, SEO services, or any other specialized service.

2. **Create Your Offering:** Define exactly what clients will get as part of your service. Be clear about the scope of work, turnaround times, and any limitations.

3. **Set Up Your Website:** Create a professional website that outlines your service, pricing, and contact information. Include testimonials and case studies to build credibility.

4. **Market Your Service:** Use social media, online ads, and content marketing to promote your service. Highlight the benefits of your productized service and showcase your success stories.

5. **Automate and Outsource:** Use tools to automate the client onboarding process and manage requests. Hire freelancers or contractors to handle specific tasks, allowing you to scale your business.

6. **Focus on Growth:** Continuously seek feedback from clients and improve your service. Focus on acquiring new clients and expanding your offerings to increase revenue.

Starting a productized service business is a smart way to turn your skills into a scalable, profitable venture. With low startup costs, high earning potential, and the ability to leverage outsourcing and automation, it's an excellent choice for aspiring entrepreneurs.

Conclusion

Congratulations! You've made it to the end of "**7 Businesses You Can Start Right Now for Under $1000.**" By now, you've explored various business opportunities that are high in ROI, low in startup costs, and packed with potential. Let's wrap things up with some final thoughts and encouragement for your journey ahead.

Recap of Key Points

Throughout this book, we've focused on practical, actionable strategies to help you start and grow your own business. Here are the key takeaways:

1. High ROI, Low-Cash Businesses: We've defined the importance of ROI and why focusing on low-cash, high-return businesses is crucial for starting with limited funds.

2. The SELL Matrix: The SELL matrix (Sellable, High Earning, Low Cost, High Leverage) is your roadmap to evaluating and choosing the right business opportunities.

3. Diverse Business Opportunities:
   a. Remote Window Cleaning: Low startup costs, high earning potential, and easy to outsource.
   b. Real Estate Listing Video Editor: High demand, minimal investment, and scalable.
   c. Microgreens Business: High profitability, easy to start, and scalable with outsourcing.
   d. Wedding Arches and Decorations Rental: Profitable market with opportunities for upsells and customization.
   e. Handyman Services: Essential services with high demand, low startup costs, and potential for outsourcing.
   f. Virtual Assistant Company: Low cost, high margin, leveraging international talent.
   g. Productized Services: Recurring revenue with a subscription model, easy to start, and scalable through outsourcing.

The Power of Acting

The most crucial step now is to take action. Reading about these opportunities is just the beginning. The real change happens when you start implementing these ideas. Remember, every successful entrepreneur started with an idea and the willingness to take that first step. Here's your blueprint—now it's time to build your future.

Encouragement for Your Journey

Starting a business is an exciting journey, but it can also be challenging. Here are a few pieces of advice to keep you motivated:

- Stay Persistent: Success doesn't happen overnight. Stay persistent, keep learning, and don't be afraid to pivot if something isn't working.

- Leverage Resources: Use the tools and platforms available to you. Whether it's finding subcontractors, marketing your services, or automating tasks, leverage technology to your advantage.

- Build Relationships: Network with other entrepreneurs, join business forums, and seek mentorship. Building relationships can open doors to new opportunities and provide valuable support.

- Keep Improving: Always look for ways to improve your business. Seek feedback from your clients, stay updated with industry trends, and continually refine your processes.

Looking Ahead

Your journey to financial freedom is just beginning. With the knowledge and strategies you've gained from this book, you're well-equipped to start your own successful business. Imagine looking back a year from now and seeing how far you've come—your life could be completely transformed.

Remember, the world is full of opportunities. Whether you choose to start a remote window cleaning business, dive into real estate video editing, grow microgreens, rent out wedding arches, offer handyman services, launch a virtual assistant company, or create a productized service, the potential for success is in your hands.

Final Thoughts

You have the power to change your life and achieve financial freedom. It all starts with taking that first step and committing to your goals. Use the strategies outlined in this book as your guide, and never stop striving for success.

Thank you for joining me on this journey. I can't wait to see what amazing things you'll accomplish. Here's to your success and the incredible future that lies ahead!

Ready to build your own castle?

Go out there and make it happen. Your future self will thank you for the effort, dedication, and perseverance you put in today. Best of luck on your entrepreneurial journey!

Dear Reader,

Thank you for reading "**7 Businesses You Can Start Right Now for Under $1000.**" If you're ready to dive deeper into achieving financial freedom, check out my book:

In "**Self-Made Success**" you'll discover:
- Inspiring stories of entrepreneurs who transformed their lives.
- Detailed strategies and actionable steps to build your own successful business.
- Insights from individuals who have successfully navigated the path to financial freedom.

Author Page

Scan The QR Code Above or Visit My **Author Page on Amazon** to Enjoy Your Copy Now.

With gratitude,

Elisabeth Miazello
https://www.amazon.com/author/elisabeth.miazello

Don't Miss Out!

Thank you for reading!
If you found this book helpful, remember to grab your **FREE eBook**:

7 Businesses to Avoid and 4 Winning Opportunities: Your Business Success Guide.

Unlock even more opportunities and take your first step towards financial freedom.

Scan the **QR Code** Above or Visit **IRNOX.com/7c** for an Instant Free Download

www.ingramcontent.com/pod-product-compliance
Lightning Source LLC
Chambersburg PA
CBHW030502220526
45464CB00006B/2619

Sampler Book 5, Ontario in Colour Photos, Saving Our History One Photo at a Time

Photography by Barbara Raué

Series Name: Cruising Ontario

Sampling from several towns

Each photo I take that precedes a demolition, or a natural disaster such as a tornado or a fire, is meeting this aim of mine of Saving Our History One Photo at a Time. There are more than 100 towns already photographed which you can visit without moving from a comfortable chair in your living room. Dream about what it was like in those by-gone days. Dream about what it was like to live in a mansion like one of these. Where would you like to travel to next?

Cover: 217 Jones Street East, St. Marys

Table of Contents

Toronto, Ontario – My Top 7 Picks

Collingwood, Ontario – My Top 9 Picks

Essex, Ontario – My Top 7 Picks

Kingsville, Ontario – My Top 12 Picks

Woodstock, Ontario – My Top 16 Picks

Thamesford, Ontario – My Top 8 Picks

St. Mary's, Ontario – My Top 13 Picks

Sarnia, Ontario – My Top 20 Picks

Petrolia, Ontario – My Top 7 Picks

Toronto, Ontario – My Top 7 Picks

Toronto, the largest city in Canada, the provincial capital of Ontario, is located in Southern Ontario on the northwestern shore of Lake Ontario. During the American Revolutionary War, United Empire Loyalists fled from the United States to live on lands north of Lake Ontario. In 1787, the British Crown purchased more than a quarter million acres of land from the Mississaugas of the New Credit, and established a settlement called the Town of York. Lieutenant Governor John Graves Simcoe designated York as the capital of Upper Canada. Fort York was constructed at the entrance of the town's natural harbor where it was sheltered by a long sand-bar peninsula. The town was captured and ransacked by American soldiers in the Battle of York during the War of 1812, and the parliament buildings were set on fire.

In 1834, York became a city and the name was changed to Toronto. In the 19th century, long-distance railway lines were constructed, including a route linking with the Upper Great Lakes. The Grand Trunk Railway and the Northern Railway of Canada joined in the building of the first Union Station. The railway brought more immigrants, and commerce and industry increased. Horse-drawn streetcars were replaced by electric ones in 1891. The great fire of 1904 destroyed a large section of downtown Toronto but the city was soon rebuilt with more stringent fire safety laws and the expansion of the fire department.

In 1954, the City of Toronto and twelve surrounding municipalities joined together into a regional government known as Metropolitan Toronto. The postwar boom resulted in rapid suburban development, and the metropolitan government began to manage services that crossed municipal boundaries, including highways, police services, water and public transit. In that year, disaster struck the city when Hurricane Hazel brought high winds and flash flooding causing the deaths of 81 people in the Toronto area, and leaving about 1,900 families homeless.

Toronto covers an area of 630 square kilometers stretching 21 kilometers (13 miles) from north to south and 43 kilometers (27 miles) east to west. The waterfront shoreline is 46 kilometers (29 miles) long. The Toronto Islands and Port Lands extend out into the lake. The city's borders are formed by Lake Ontario to the south, Etobicoke Creek and Highway 427 to the west, Steeles Avenue to the north and the Rouge River and the Scarborough-Pickering Townline to the east. Today the city has a population of 2.6 million people.

The city is intersected by three rivers and many tributaries: the Humber River in the west end and the Don River east of downtown, and the Rouge River at the city's eastern limits. The many creeks and rivers created large tracts of densely forested ravines, and provided sites for parks and recreational trails.

Toronto is a city of high-rises with 1,800 buildings over 30 metres (98 feet), most of them are residential having been built in the 1950s, while the central business district contains commercial office towers.